D1358716

This book is dedicated to John Klopp, my spectacular husband,
who has encouraged and supported me
throughout many projects and productions
during our well-lived life together.
He is my very best traveling buddy.

What 2 Wear Where
Packing for Travel
Karen Klopp

Published by Karen Klopp and What2WearWhere.com

Find us on the Web at www.What2WearWhere.com
To report errors, please send a note to info@What2WearWhere.com

ISBN 978-0-9966604-0-2

WHAT2WEARWHERE.COM

Packing for Travel

From jetset to trekset, the definitive globe-trotting guide

Karen Klopp, Founder of What2WearWhere.com

Illustrations by Lara Glaister

TABLE OF CONTENTS

TABLE OF CONTENTS

INTRODUCTION

"The journey of a thousand miles begins with a single step."

Lao Tzu, ancient Chinese philosopher

This is the book that will help you take that single step, packing for travel. Just the word, **packing**, can send one into fits of panic and palpitations, but we are here to lay it out in simple steps that will save you time and confusion. You can trust the **What2WearWhere** tried and true motto: *We take the guesswork out of dressing, the legwork out of shopping and the panic out of packing.*

Some say that they hate to travel, but when probed, they will admit that it is packing that they dread. Others take the "throw it all in" approach. Ouch, that hurts! We find that if you are organized, thoughtful, and selective in the process, you can arrive at your destination confident with everything you need to enjoy your holiday, whether for business, pleasure, or a little of both.

To best use this book, read the beginning chapters for a general overview of our packing philosophy, and then turn to the sections that interest you and fit your travel needs. Use the blank packing list pages in the back to map out your needs and activities for upcoming destinations. And, of course, contact us with your specific destination questions and we will get back to you with our stylish suggestions.

Let's get started, the world is waiting for you!

xxoohh

Chapter 1
How to Pack

Plan Your Travel Wardrobe

10 Top Travel Essentials

10 Steps to Panic Free Packing

Packing Lists

The Basics | Exercise Wear | Jewelry | Toiletries

Packing Techniques

How Long? How Much?

PLAN YOUR TRAVEL WARDROBE

What to Look For in a Travel Wardrobe?
When shopping, look for stylish clothes that won't wrinkle, and think in terms of **layers. Knits** are ideal; choose **cotton for warmer** climates and **wool for colder** ones, especially with a little stretchy content like **Lycra**. There was a time when elegant ladies wouldn't be caught dead in the dreaded polyester. Now we call them synthetics, and they are a traveler's best friend. You can wear a garment again and again, and it will look fresh and wrinkle-free. It is important to remember that these fabrics tend to be hotter than natural fibers, so when going to any sort of tropical climate, it is a good idea to mix with linens and cottons.

Leather and suede are useful, year-round travel fabrics. They create a timelessly chic look that is comfortable and endlessly wearable. To clean leather, simply wipe it off. For suede, use a brush to keep it looking fresh.

For colder destinations, **fur and faux fur** are ideal for style, warmth, and versatility.

Pick a **stylish tote** to carry on the plane, and to use as your daytime bag upon arrival at your destination. Make sure the bag coordinates with the rest of your wardrobe. We like black and neutral shades, but a punch of color can make a personal statement.

Today's **lightweight down vests and jackets** are a woman's coziest travel friend. They are easy to pack, as they scrunch down to nothing, and are useful in every climate.

10 TOP TRAVEL ESSENTIALS

#1. Pashmina or Wrap. It is a Godsend on the plane and at your destination for both day and night, folding small enough to carry in your bag and providing a cozy bit of luxury away from home.

#1a. Lightweight Down Vest. Yes, even in the heat of the summer, you will be surprised at how useful this travel essential can be.

#2. Black, Dark Blue or White Stretch Jeans, depending on the season. The darker jeans have a more formal look, and are universally stylish. Ditto for the white ones in warm climates.

#3. Comfortable Shoes. Nothing worse than sore feet when traveling. Also pack some **Gel Beds** and a **Friction Stick**.

#4. Stylish Tote Bag. For both on the plane, and carrying by day to keep your essentials together neatly, and picking up some choice souvenirs.

#5. Cocktail Dress. You never know when an opportunity arises to wear it. Last minute invitation? Impromptu Drinks Party? Take a light knit that is easy to pack.

#6. High Heel Pumps or **Sandals**. See **#5**

#7. Lightweight Statement Jewelry. It can change your look in minutes.

#8. What2WearWhere Travel Bags, The Bags That Pack Themselves.™ See page 21 for details.

#9. Paperback Book. In case of flight delays with no internet or Wifi.

#10. Sense of Humor. It can get you through the inevitable travel challenges with style.

10 STEPS TO PANIC-FREE PACKING

Step 1. Hello, Social Calendar! Make a list of events you will be attending. Plan a well-thought-out travel wardrobe by making a list of the events or activities that you are likely to engage in during your travels. We have included some blank worksheets in the back of the book for you to use for planning.

Examples:
- **On the Plane**: black knit pants, turtleneck, scarf, boots, trench, tote
- **Museum Hopping**: black knit pants, blouse, cardigan, flats, tote
- **Lunch with Aunt Lizzie**: skirt, boots, blouse, cardigan, purse
- **Tea with the Queen**: dress, cardigan, pumps, hat, gloves, purse
- **Cocktails with old Beau**: black pants, low-cut sequin sweater, pumps, clutch

Step 2. Spin the Color Wheel. It is very helpful to decide in advance on your color scheme and stick to it. That way you can interchange your shoes and accessories, making your outfits all coordinate beautifully. You can also rely on neutrals, such as khaki, black and white, and then pick several accent colors which will punch up your outfits.

Some of our favorite color palettes for warm climates:
- Black, White, Hot Pink
- Blue, Tan, Brown
- Orange, Pink, Peach
- Blue, Aqua, Green

Some suggestions for cooler weather:
- Black, Grey, Purple or Royal Blue
- Winter White, Cream, Camel
- Burgundy, Dusty Pink, Black
- Hunter Green, Camel, Brown

10 STEPS TO PANIC-FREE PACKING

Step 3. Gotcha Covered. Use the Packing Lists throughout the book and the blank lists in the back to keep track of packing. You will always want to start with: **What to Pack On the Plane, Basic Packing List,** and **Essential Toiletries List**

Step 4. Ready for Anything. Track the weather at www.weather.com

Don't be caught off guard by a sudden change in weather. Keep checking until the last minute. Then add or subtract more layers as the temperature warrants.

Step 5. To Check or To Carry? That is the Question. Decide whether you will check your luggage or use a carry on bag. This decision is key in guiding your wardrobe selections. Remember, it is NOT a good idea to over pack a suitcase as it makes for a miserable experience when you have to unpack and repack. But if you are thoughtful and plan ahead, you will make everything fit. See **Page 37** for a list of what fits in a carry on bag.

Step 6. Edit, Edit, Edit. This is a very important step. Lay your clothes out on a bed and see how they coordinate. **Try everything on**, especially if you are packing out of season clothing. Then edit your choices well, making sure you will wear each item at least twice. This is the time to make the hard decisions on what to let go. If you have pared down as far as you comfortably can, and you can't fit it all into a bag, you may have to consider a larger case.

If space allows, pack an additional lightweight tote that folds flat for any serious shopping escapades and souvenirs.

10 STEPS TO PANIC-FREE PACKING

Step 7. Sure You Have Everything? Check your selections against the **Packing Lists**, making sure you have all that you need. It is easier to pack an item than trying to find it when you arrive. Even the simplest incidentals can be elusive when you are in unfamiliar territory.

Step 8. Meds R' Us. Pack all of your medications in the bag you carry onboard. Remember to fill any prescriptions you might need in an emergency. Check with your doctor or **CDC.gov** for required vaccinations. If you wear contacts, always bring an extra few pairs, just in case.

Step 9. Bring Bling. Pack your jewelry bag in your carry on, not in your checked luggage. It is a personal choice whether you like to travel with precious jewelry or substitute with costume jewels and less valuable pieces. After losing several pieces of our favorites, we found the latter to be very practical. A good rule of thumb is to **"Never travel with any piece whose disappearance would mar your holiday."**

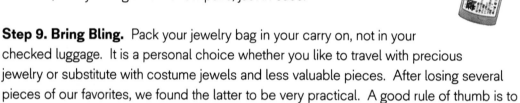

Step 10. Be Prepared. Copy your travel documents electronically and also make a paper copy of your passport ID page, driver's license, airline tickets, hotel reservations, car rental agreements, and credit cards. It is a good idea to have a paper copy in case modern technology fails. Make sure that someone has a copy of your itinerary back home.

ALL THE BASICS TO PACK

THE BASICS
These are the items that you will need for every trip. Even though they seem like the obvious choices, we like to point them out to avoid missing essentials. Yes, it is possible to leave your knickers behind. Make sure you look at your wardrobe to bring the **appropriate undergarments**. If you are packing knits, you will need a seamless bra and perhaps some shapewear, slip or shorts. We always pack a strapless bra for our dresses to create a clean neckline.

BASICS PACKING LIST
- ○ panties (1 per day plus 2 extras)
- ○ 2 bras
- ○ strapless bra
- ○ camisole
- ○ shapewear or slip
- ○ socks
- ○ stockings or tights
- ○ pajamas or night gown
- ○ robe
- ○ slippers or flip-flops

If you are planning on wearing lots of white and cream shades of clothing, keep your undies in the neutral range.

PACK TO EXERCISE

EXERCISE CLOTHING
This will depend on the time of year and your **workout preference**: whether you like an early morning run, a workout in the gym or in your room, or a swim in a pool.

EXERCISE CLOTHING PACKING LIST

- ○ bathing suit, bathing cap, goggles
- ○ sports bra
- ○ shorts or exercise pants
- ○ wicking t-shirt or tank
- ○ socks
- ○ sneakers or exercise shoes

COLD WEATHER ADD-ONS
- ○ polar fleece vest
- ○ light weight jacket
- ○ gloves
- ○ hat
- ○ gator

PACKABLE EQUIPMENT
There are some very good options that don't take up much room in your bag. TV and online Fitness Programs are good alternatives when traveling.
- ○ resistance bands & loops
- ○ balance disc
- ○ jump rope

We often pack Fit-Flops or Tevas instead of sneakers as they pack flat and are great for brisk exercise walks.

PACKING JEWELRY

JEWELRY

We have picked the minimum number of pieces to pack. Obviously you can add to this list depending on your needs and your events list. We find lightweight statement jewelry provides great impact and takes up little space in your bag. There are many useful jewelry bags on the market. Find the one that works for your travel collection.

JEWELRY PACKING LIST - DAY

- ○ hoop earrings
- ○ small studs
- ○ chain bracelet
- ○ pendant necklace
- ○ casual watch

JEWELRY PACKING LIST - NIGHT

- ○ statement earrings
- ○ big cuff
- ○ dramatic necklace
- ○ dress watch

Often local shopping will turn up the best discoveries in decorative pieces to wear, and they are wonderful keepsakes of your trip.

TOTAL TOILETRIES

Stash in small sizes! If you travel very often, it's a good idea to have a basic kit ready to go. Don't forget our **W2WW Travel Bags, The Bags That Pack Themselves.™** Each perfectly sized bag comes stocked with products and packing lists.

While many hotels provide basics like **shampoos** and **conditioner**, we feel more secure when we travel with our own products. The same goes with small appliances, like hair dryers, curling irons and so forth. Don't forget to **follow the details of the list,** checking off items you have packed, and ignoring any items that you don't need. It can be annoying to forget small things like tweezers and nail clippers, only to discover their absence just when you find a stray hair or hang-nail.

TOTAL TOILETRIES

PERSONAL ITEMS

- O eye cream, face cream
- O face wash
- O sunscreen & lip protection
- O body lotion
- O makeup remover
- O q-tips, cotton balls or wipes
- O eye drops
- O contact lenses & solution
- O toothbrush & toothpaste
- O floss or picks
- O perfume
- O feminine hygiene products
- O contraceptives, lubricant, stimulators

HAIR, NAILS & FEET

- O shampoo & conditioner
- O setting lotion & mousse
- O hair spray
- O comb & brush
- O hair ties, clips, pins, rollers
- O hair sunscreen
- O shower cap
- O small folding hairdryer
- O curling iron or straightening wand
- O clip on pony tail or hair piece
- O adaptors if traveling abroad
- O nail clipper & tweezers
- O small scissors
- O razor and shave cream or other hair removal products
- O nail file & maintenance products
- O nail polish & remover
- O friction stick
- O gel beds for shoes

TOTAL TOILETRIES

HEALTH

- O prescription medication
- O pain reliever
- O antacid, anti-nausea medicine
- O bandaids & antiseptic
- O antibacterial wipes & spray
- O laxative or cleansing tea bags
- O vitamins

MISCELLANEOUS

- O bug repellent
- O sewing kit
- O small folding umbrella
- O lighted travel mirror
- O small flashlight
- O spare batteries for electronics
- O rain poncho or travel trench
- O hand and feet warmers
- O plastic Ziploc® bags
- O binoculars
- O art supplies

It is a good idea to pack a few gallon Ziploc® bags. They come in handy for worn underwear, wet bathing suits and so many other uses.

Use a Friction Stick on overnight flights, and your shoes will glide back on upon your arrival. Apply it daily to avoid tired feet from walking and standing.

W2WW Travel Bags

Don't forget to check out our **What2WearWhere Travel Bags, The Bags That Pack Themselves** (TM).

What2WearWhere's worldwide wanderers, **Hilary Dick, Leslie Johnson,** and **Karen Klopp,** have created a top of the line set of travel bags, offering savvy solutions to the challenges of packing. Tired of looking for the perfect travel bags, they designed these bags for foolproof travel.

Each attractive bag is made of waterproof raffia, chicly piped with shiny black patent and lined in the hot, hot, hottest shade of pink. Bags may be purchased empty or stocked with indispensable beauty products. Each contains a laminated **W2WW Packing Lists** for total packing ease.

Bag of Tricks holds cosmetics and makeup. The **Hair Brain** packs hair dryer, shampoo, conditioners, brushes and anything related to our tresses. The **Oh La La** is for your personal items such as lubricants, vaginal cleansing cloths, and contraceptives. It is also a perfect small case for all of your travel jewelry.

For more information and to purchase please go to: **What2WearWhere.com**

10 STEP PACKING TECHNIQUES

To start, read our chapter on **Panic Free Packing**. Once you have the basics down, you are ready to roll or fold or fill, depending on your style.

Step 1. Lay out all of your clothes, shoes, accessories and toiletries beside your suitcase, straps on the outside. Make sure to lay out your "on the plane" outfit. Try to wear and carry your bulkiest items, a coat and boots, for example.

Step 2. To roll, fold or pack in sacs? The **"roll"** is generally used for more casual vacationing and adventure travel, and it helps to maximize the space in your suitcase. Some travelers prefer the simple **"fold"** while others like to **"pack in sacs,"** organizing neatly and folding by type.

Step 3. How to Roll: Fold dresses and tops with face up, and fold the sleeves or sides in towards the middle. Then starting at one end, roll tightly almost like a sleeping bag. For pants and shorts, fold them in half lengthwise, one leg on top of the other and then roll. Some like to use large rubber bands to keep the rolls neat.

Step 4. How to Fold: Lay clothing out flat. For dress and shirts, place face down. Fold the sleeves and about 2" of the item, in towards the middle, keeping lines straight. Then fold the bottom up to meet the top. **Dresses** will need an additional fold – so fold up a third from the bottom and then down from the top. **For pants**, keeping side seams straight, fold along the front crease, or create one. Fold in half or thirds, depending on your case size. Some people like to layer tissue or dry cleaner plastic bags between items to keep them wrinkle free. This is also a good place for empty **Ziploc®** bags that will come in handy later in the trip.

10 Step Packing Techniques

Step 5. How to Pack in Sacs: First fold your items as described in Step 4. Then stack all of the similar items on top of each other. Carefully place stacks into individual packing sacs, either fabric, mesh or plastic. This method keeps items together, and your suitcase neat and organized. It works really well if you are traveling from place to place, and unable to unpack at a destination. But remember, for the system to work efficiently, **you must keep it organized** and return items to their proper sac. Friends rave about **Compression Bags** which have an one way valve that forces the air out thus reducing space.

Step 6. Save on Space: Tuck smaller items into larger ones, like belts into shoes, or scarfs into clutch bags, socks into sneakers.

Step 7. Act of Packing: The trick in packing is pure geometry – try to use every available square inch of the case.

If you are folding, we like to start with slacks on the bottom. Then place your pile of pants on the left side of the bag, and the stack of dresses and tops on the right. You will have created a moat-like space around the clothing. Into the side spaces, tuck your shoes (soles turned away from clothing), clutch, and other accessories. Put your underwear in the spaces in the middle that are left on the sides, or on top of the clothing. Place **two empty Ziploc® bags** over the clothing, and then add your toiletry kit or kits on top. On top of this put something soft, like a down vest or a sweater to pad the top of the suitcase. Check to make sure the case is **balanced**, and you are ready to zip and go.

If you are rolling, we suggest putting shoes and toiletries on the bottom of your case, then stack rolls on top, layering as you go. Fill in any gaps with accessories until you have packed the entire case.

If you are packing in sacs, layer them flat, starting on the bottom. Wedge shoes and accessories around the outer edge and on top of the sacs, leaving room in the middle to lay your toiletries. Cover with pouch containing sweaters or other soft items.

PACKING TECHNIQUES

Step 8. Everything Fit? No? Hate this! If after following these instructions, you find you cannot fit all of your items in your case, look at the bulky items to remove. Can you function

without your sneakers and take flip flops instead, can you wear your boots on the plane, or can you eliminate a sweater? We understand that these are hard choices. So if the answer is "no" then you will have to take a bigger bag or an additional bag. If we have the space, we take a folding tote, like **Le Pliage by Longchamp.** It proves useful on the return trip after acquiring a

few delectable trinkets and treasures. It also solves a traveling phenomena – clean folded clothes take up less space than dirty ones. Don't know why!

Step 9. Speaking of dirty clothes. The two large **Ziploc®** bags that you packed come in handy for worn undies and wet things when packing between destinations or on the return trip.

Step 10. Moment of truth! If you are checking your bag, weigh it – either on your bathroom scale, or on a luggage scale. Your weight limit, without incurring excess fees, is 50 pounds or 23kg. It is good to know if you have exceeded before you arrive at the airport. It avoids unpleasant surprises at check in.

See Page 31 for what to pack in a carry on bag. With thoughtful planning, you can make everything fit.

HOW LONG? HOW MUCH?

The **Packing Lists** in this book are based on get-aways from **5 to 7 days**, but in truth you could go **10 days** or more on most them. Once you have the basics, you don't really have to add much more to stay in a destination for a longer period of time. **Our Lists** are meant to include every possibility for packing. You can modify them to suit your own personal needs. Of course, it is very much dependent on where you are going and the range of activities.

But if you take our advice on packing **clothes that breathe and stretch**, you can wear your clothing multiple times without washing. As a rule, we wash our undies whenever we land in a place for two or more days. And don't forget to fold or hang your clothing to keep it fresh and wrinkle free.

These pieces are fabulous wardrobe stretchers. **Black Cropped Pants, Print Knit Dress, Silk Blouse, and Cardigan Sweater.**

CHAPTER 2
ON THE PLANE

What to Wear On Board

What to Carry

Luggage Guide

To Check or Not To Check

WHAT TO WEAR ON BOARD

Lucky you! You are on your way to a travel destination, adventure, or business trip. The voyage begins **on the plane,** so dress for it. No sneakers please – and no exercise clothing, pajama-looking-things, or shorts. We have all seen our fair share of inadvisable travel wear, and have concluded that there is no reason to look anything but chic and stylish. Start with items that have a little **stretch**, such as **knits**. **Cotton knits** work well in the **summer**. Think of **wools** and heavier fabrics when traveling to and from **cooler climates**. Wear **trousers** with some **lycra**, a **knit top** paired with a **jacket** or a **cardigan**. We cannot overemphasize the importance of layering, as cabin temperatures can be chilly even in the summer. It is a good idea to wear your bulkiest items on the plane.

For footwear, we suggest **ballet flats, wedges, kitten heels,** or **low-heeled boots** for comfort. Don't forget a **pashmina** and a **tote** for all of your carry on essentials.

Never travel without a pashmina or wrap, it can function as a blanket, a pillow, or as a cozy escape from a pushy seatmate.

WEAR ON BOARD

- O   knit top
- O   pants with lycra
- O   blazer or cardigan
- O   light jacket, trench coat, or temperature appropriate outerwear
- O   ballet flats, wedges, kitten heels or low-heeled boots

ACCESSORIES

- O   pashmina or wrap
- O   lightweight down vest
- O   tote bag
- O   simple jewelry

Turn the page to see our suggestions for what to pack in your **On Board Tote Bag**.

If you are flying from a cold climate to a warmer one, or the reverse, wear or bring a pair of tights, then add or remove them mid-flight.

TOTE ON BOARD

As we know, the airlines are getting strict on the **number of bags you can carry** on a plane. If you are planning to place your luggage in the overhead compartment, you are allowed one other bag. This bag should be a **great looking, sturdy tote**. It will become your day bag at your destination, so factor it in when you are looking at your wardrobe. Black, tan, grey, whatever the shade, make sure it will coordinate with the rest of your things.

Current TSA and Airline Regulations aka the 3-1-1:
3: All liquids, gels, and aerosols must be in 3.4 ounce (100ml) or smaller containers. Larger containers that are half-full or toothpaste tubes rolled up are not allowed.

1: All liquids, gels, and aerosols must be placed in a single, quart size, ziptop, clear plastic bag. Gallon size bags, or bags that are not ziptop, such as fold-over sandwich bags, are not allowed. Each traveler can use only one, quart size, ziptop, clear plastic bag.

1: Each traveler must remove their quart-sized plastic, ziptop bag from the carry on and place it in a bin or on the conveyor belt for X-ray screening to allow TSA security officers to more easily examine the declared items.

Although we all love reading on our tablets, it is important to travel with a printed book in case you are stuck on the plane and not permitted to "turn on."

Pack your chargers, adaptors and cords in a clear plastic bag. Use cord ties to keep everything organized. Charge your devices whenever you have a chance.

Onboard Packing List

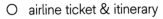

- O airline ticket & itinerary
- O drivers license, passport & visas
- O wallet
- O medication
- O antibacterial wipes for seat & tray
- O saline solution, nasal spray, or neosporin to dab in each nostril
- O eyedrops, contact lenses & case
- O make up, moisurizer, & face wipes
- O eye mask & ear plugs
- O toothpaste & toothbrush
- O tissues

- O small hairbrush or comb
- O sunglasses & case
- O eye glasses & case
- O cell phone, charger & external battery
- O laptop, tablet, iPod & chargers
- O electrical adaptor, if traveling abroad
- O earphone & earbuds
- O camera & charger
- O day book or small notebook & pen
- O business cards
- O reading material: book, magazines, guide book

- O money in the currency of your destination
- O pashmina or other wrap
- O slippers or socks for long flights
- O jewelry bag
- O snacks
- O empty, reusable water bottle to fill after security
- O feminine wipes & panty liners
- O small hydrating spray

LUGGAGE

Wheels down! For our personal luggage choices, we prefer **bags with wheels** which make maneuvering airports and transportation hubs manageable. Wheeled bags have been a boon to women traveling alone. It feels good to roll along, totally self-sufficient in your dash through interminable terminals.

Take a good look at your luggage. If it was your college graduation gift, it may be time for a change. Do you like it? Does it really suit you?

Bags are an important part of your travel ensemble, reflecting your personal style. There are some excellent choices available now, and you don't have to spend a fortune. If you are looking for a new bag or bags, look for a design that comes in different sizes and shapes, so you can mix and match, depending on your destination. **Durability, expandability, and organizational pockets** are other important features.

Take a test drive when shopping for luggage. Make sure the handles are properly positioned and the rolling features are high quality.

LUGGAGE

Here are the **5 bag shapes** that should be in everyone's luggage collection, whether you like a matched set or more of a mixed bag effect.

1. Rectangular Carry on Bag.
For casual holidays, short jaunts, weekend trips.

2. Larger Rectangle Bag.
For longer trips, urban destinations, business trips.

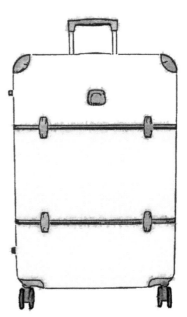

3. Rolling Duffel Bag.

For casual holidays, exotic, and remote destinations and safaris.

4. Suit or Dress Bag.

For any destination where you plan on attending an event, with a long formal dress or for business trips.

5. Computer Bag.

We find this size handy when taking a laptop and all of your electronics (it even fits a portable printer). It's also great for files, books, and magazines.

LUGGAGE

Guidelines for Luggage Dimension for U.S. Airlines/Domestic:

Your carry on bag cannot be larger than **45 inches** when you combine the length, width, and height. The maximum weight varies by airline, so it is best to check.

For your checked luggage, it cannot be larger than **62 inches** when you combine length, width, and height. The weight cannot exceed **50 pounds** each.

International Airlines generally follow the same guidelines, but check with your carrier to be sure.

Make sure your luggage has secure ID tags on it both inside and outside. Luggage locks have to be TSA-approved or may be cut off by security.

To Check or Not To Check

To Check or Not To Check?

It is such a breeze to be able to roll right onto the plane and stow your luggage in the overhead. The trick is to board the plane before all of the overhead compartments are full. In this case, they take your bag from you. **Have you ever seen a grown woman cry?** All of your precise packing and planning goes right out the window, or in this case, down below in the luggage compartment. And you are stuck watching and waiting by the carousel. Here are some tips to help.

Tip #1. It is worth the price to pay a little more to board early, if the service is available.

Tip #2. Keep up to date with your **Airline Mileage Clubs**. They may offer an early board perk for member loyalty.

Tip #3. Get to the airport, and to your gate in **plenty of time**.

Tip #4. Stand when the boarding begins so you are one of the **first to board** when your section is announced.

Tip #5. Most airlines limit bags to one overhead and one under the seat, so **plan accordingly**.

Long delay? Many Airline Clubs have a day rate to use their facilities. If you have a long layover or flight delay, it may be worth the fee.

WHAT FITS IN A CARRY ON

WHAT FITS IN A STANDARD CARRY ON BAG?

- ○ 3 tops
- ○ 2 slacks
- ○ 1 cardigan
- ○ 1 cocktail dress
- ○ 1 day dress
- ○ 1 bathing suit & cover up
- ○ 1 set of exercise clothes
- ○ 1 pair of travel sneakers or fitflops
- ○ 1 pair of flats
- ○ 1 pair of heels
- ○ 1 nightgown: use the hotel robe
- ○ undies & stockings
- ○ jewelry
- ○ toiletry bag
- ○ scarf or wrap

To simplify passing through security, we strongly recommend obtaining a Global Entry Card. Visit cbp.gov/globalentry for details.

CHAPTER 3
ON THE TOWN

Warm Weather

Cold Weather

Business Travel

WARM WEATHER

When traveling in cities, you will want to pack your smartest of styles, streamlining your choices, but not at the expense of fashion. Whether your destination is **Buenos Aires, Dubai, Hong Kong, or Berlin**, our first stop is **weather.com** to find out what to expect. It is also our last stop, checking back right before the flight to make sure there are no storms or fronts heading in at the last minute. Even in the warmest weather, take a **sweater and wrap** along with you for the chilly air conditioned interiors.

It is so fantastic to see the far and near corners of the world and to experience other cultures firsthand. It is important to check local conventions when traveling abroad to make sure you **respect the traditions of your host country.** For instance, if your holiday takes you to the Middle East, of course you are not expected to wear a burka, but on the same hand, we wouldn't recommend an outfit that is short, tight or revealing. Another example, as a visitor to the Vatican in Rome, you will not be permitted to enter St. Peter's in shorts, but we don't recommend shorts for sightseeing anyway. **If you are in doubt, please contact us and we will get back to you, with proper attire for your destination.**

*Ciao bella!
Read up on your destination, Google it and ask us. We have correspondents around the globe, ready to help.*

WARM WEATHER | PACKING LIST

DAYWEAR

- O 2 tops
- O 2 day dresses
- O 1 pair of white jeans or pants
- O 1 skirt
- O 1 cardigan sweater
- O 1 light jacket or blazer
- O 1 light trench coat

EVENING WEAR

- O 2 evening tops
- O 1 pair of white pants
- O 2 cocktail dresses

SHOES

- O 1 pair of comfortable shoes or sandals
- O 1 pair of platform or flat form wedges
- O 1 pair of high heeled sandals

ACCESSORIES

- O 1 or 2 wraps or pashminas
- O 1 belt
- O 1 tote for day
- O 1 clutch for evening
- O jewelry
- O sun hat
- O sunglasses

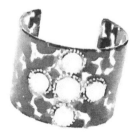

COLD WEATHER

There is no such thing as bad weather, just bad clothing. We couldn't agree more. Winter travel can be brisk and invigorating, provided you know how to pack for it. The fabrics we love are **wool** and **cashmere knits, suede,** and **leather,** and **fur** or **faux fur**. They also happen to create a fantastically chic look for colder climates. Think in terms of layers so you are prepared for sudden changes in weather.

When traveling in the cold we love to wear **a sweater dress, scarf, tights and boots**, topped with a **puffer coat.** An alternative is **pants, turtleneck sweater, scarf and a fur or faux fur vest**. **Hats and gloves** are a must. **Cashmere scarves** are a wonderful way to keep your neck warm while adding a pop of color and pattern to a muted winter ensemble. For all the walking that you will be doing, we like low **heeled or wedged boots** to keep your feet toasty.

We often pack silk long underwear as a base layer. It is thin and luxurious to keep you toasty without the bulk.

COLD WEATHER | PACKING LIST

DAYWEAR

- ○ 2 tops
- ○ 1 cardigan sweater
- ○ 1 turtleneck sweater
- ○ 1 sweater dress
- ○ 1 pair of dark jeans or pants
- ○ 1 vest: fur, faux or down
- ○ 1 warm coat: down, fur, wool
- ○ thin thermal underwear

EVENING WEAR

- ○ 2 evening tops
- ○ 1 pair of black pants
- ○ 2 cocktail dresses

SHOES

- ○ 1 pair of low heeled boots
- ○ 1 pair of high heeled boots
- ○ 1 pair of pumps

ACCESSORIES

- ○ 1 or 2 wraps or pashminas
- ○ 1 belt
- ○ 1 hat & gloves
- ○ 1 tote for day
- ○ 1 clutch for evening
- ○ jewelry
- ○ sunglasses

BUSINESS TRAVEL

Business travel can be a wonderful and productive experience, provided you are not stressing about what to pack, so arrive with everything you need to hit the ground running. Savvy professionals pride themselves on the worthy goal of never checking luggage. To achieve this, start with picking key pieces – **blazer or jacket, pants, pencil skirt, LBD.** Then choose the proper separates to mix and match for head to toe, day to night style – **tops, cardigans, scarves or pashminas.** The key is to put together the right combination for maximum flexibility.

Whether you work in a **corporate** position or a **creative** one, we recommend **black** or **navy** as your **base colors**. Both are universally acceptable in business and social situations. Remember traveling always starts with dressing for the plane where it is important to **wear your heavier pieces onboard,** saving room in your carry on bag. We recommend packing **separates** that are made with fabrics that have a touch of stretch to maintain a fresh wrinkle-free look.

BUSINESS TRAVEL | PACKING LIST

5 Day Wardrobe

- O 1 jacket/blazer
- O 1 pencil skirt
- O 1 pairs of pants with stretch
- O 1 cardigan
- O 1 little black dress
- O 2 tops: 1 blouse, 1 camisole
- O 1 trench coat

Accessories

- O 1 pashmina
- O 2 scarves
- O 1 tote or work bag
- O 1 clutch
- O jewelry

Shoes

- O 1 pair of ballet flats or wedges
- O 1 pair of kitten heels
- O 1 pair of high heels

CHAPTER 4
BEACH, BOAT AND CLUB

Resort

On Deck

Cruise

Tennis

Golf

RESORT

Getting away to a **tropical destination**? Ah, just listen to the sound of the water, lapping the shores. If only everything was as easy as life at a beach resort – whether you're in **St. Barth's**, **Phuket**, or **Punta del Este**, dressing for the beach is ecstatically easy: a **bathing suit, cover up** and **sandals** can take you from sunup to sundown. Crisp **white pants** and a sensational **tunic**, or a **long flowing dress** are perfect for an elegant evening by the water. Sometimes the most simple trips can present the greatest packing challenge and so, to avoid a hodge podge of fashion, we have a list to help you **organize your wardrobe planning.**

Our lovely seaside color combos:

 Sea Blues – various shades of blue, green and white paired with sparkling silver accessories.

 Pink Sandy Beaches – peach, orange, pinks and creams with warm golden accessories.

 Eastern Seaboard – the tried and true red, white and blue with bright gold accents.

 Simply White – just that! It is a dream to pack for especially for some of the locations where temperatures can really sizzle.

RESORT | PACKING LIST

DAY

- O 2 bathing suits
- O 2 cover ups or sarongs
- O 1 sun dress
- O 1 pair of shorts or skirt
- O 2 casual tops
- O 1 light cardigan
- O 1 light waterproof jacket

EVENING

- O 2 evening tops or tunics
- O 2 pairs of white jeans or pants
- O 3 cocktail dresses, long or short
- O 1 wrap or pashmina

SHOES

- O 1 pair of comfortable shoes for walking
- O 1 pair flat sandals or flip flops
- O 1 pair of platform or flatform wedges
- O 1 pair of strappy sandals

ACCESSORIES

- O wrap or pashmina
- O sunglasses
- O sun hat
- O tote for day
- O clutch for evenings
- O small waterproof bag for phone & camera
- O jewelry

On Deck

Whether you are on a **yacht or a yawl**, it is most essential to pack efficiently while taking everything that you may need for a wonderful holiday on the sea. Space to stow your gear is most likely compact, so it is important to organize a shipshape wardrobe, coordinating your color choices. You have to be prepared for **hot, sunny days** lounging on deck, **exploring** port towns, maybe even a bit of **hiking**. Nights and some days on board can be chilly when the wind picks up, so bring a few warmer things.

Daywear will be a breeze! A simple **bathing suit** paired with **cover ups**, **sundresses** for on land explorations and a pair of **sandals**. A nautical necessity is a **small waterproof bag** for your camera and phone.

Evenings call for **white jeans** with a **festive top**, sandals or espadrille wedges and a clutch if going ashore. Pack a wrinkle proof **cocktail dress** just in case, and as always, a **cozy wrap** is essential.

Always carry a tote for sunscreen, hat, book, phone, etc. Even for lounging on deck. Best to keep everything together – shipshape!

ON DECK | PACKING LIST

DAY

- ○ 3 bathing suits
- ○ 3 cover ups or sarongs
- ○ 2 t-shirts, tank-tops or lightweight shirts
- ○ 1 pair of shorts or skirt
- ○ 1 sweater or fleece
- ○ 1 rash guard & pair of lycra shorts for kayaking & boarding

EVENING

- ○ 2 evening tops or tunics
- ○ 2 pairs of white jeans or capris
- ○ 2 dresses: long or short

SHOES

- ○ 1 pair of rubber-soled shoes or sandals
- ○ 1 pair of water shoes or sport sandals
- ○ 1 pair of wedge sandals
- ○ 1 pair of platform sandals

ACCESSORIES

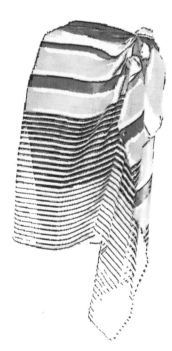

- ○ sunglasess
- ○ 1 pashmina or wrap
- ○ 1 tote
- ○ 1 clutch
- ○ 1 small waterproof bag
- ○ 1 sun hat
- ○ jewelry
- ○ 1 quilted vest
- ○ 1 waterproof jacket

CRUISE

Cruise Ships come in all shapes and sizes as do the attire recommendations and requirements. Along with our suggestions, it is best to check your cruise line for their packing recommendations. Many cruises have a **formal dress policy** of **Black Tie** for evenings, so if the idea of this is not your cup of tea, you might want to keep looking for other cruise carriers.

For **onboard daywear**, boats are casual with **swimsuits and cover ups** as the catch of the day. We like to suggest coordinating colors or patterns for covering up to go from lounge deck to lunch deck with ease.

On **land excursions** you will be sightseeing and exploring, and for this we like a **sundress** or **skirt** and **light top**, with **sandals** that are comfortable when walking.

Whether on land or sea, you will want to carry a **tote or pack** to handle all of your essentials such as sunscreen, hat, books, guide books, camera, cell phone, and a water bottle.

In the evening, if the attire is not formal, think **Resort Chic.** This will call for **white jeans** and a **tunic top,** or a colorful **cocktail dress**. When the attire is **Formal** or **Black Tie**, you can wear an elegant long dress or a short festive one, then simply add **high-heeled sandals** or **evening shoes** and some special jewelry. You will need a **wrap** for the evening chill on deck and the air conditioned salons.

CRUISE | PACKING LIST

DAYWEAR
- ○ 3 swimsuits
- ○ 3 cover ups & sarongs
- ○ 2 tops
- ○ 1 pair of shorts or skirt
- ○ 1 day dresses
- ○ 1 cardigan sweater
- ○ 1 pair of lycra shorts
- ○ 1 SPF 50 rash guard for water activities

EVENING WEAR
- ○ 2 evening tops or tunics
- ○ 2 pairs of white jeans or pants
- ○ 2 long or short dresses
- ○ 2 formal dresses: optional

SHOES
- ○ 1 pair of sandals or flip flops
- ○ 1 pair of platform sandals
- ○ 1 pair of high-heeled sandals

ACCESSORIES
- ○ 2 pashminas or wraps
- ○ 1 tote
- ○ 1 clutch
- ○ 1 small waterproof bag
- ○ sunglasses
- ○ 1 hat
- ○ jewelry
- ○ 1 waterproof jacket

TENNIS

Love – you! We can't resist a sport you start scoring at "love," and where the clothes look as classically chic as a **Ralph Lauren** advertisement. Early women players popularized the **white tennis apparel** trend because the clothes reflected sunlight and masked perspiration, and this became the required shade in clubs of that time.

Many tennis clubs still adhere to this policy, while others will allow **a bit of color** in the trim, and some have **no set requirements**, so it is best to check before you go. The new wicking fabrics make comfortable and stylish clothes that **dry quickly** and look fresh all day. Start with a good **sports bra**; add a **shirt**, **skirt** or **shorts,** or **tennis dress**. **Tennis shoes** with good construction and support will keep you on your toes. Make sure the sneakers have non-marking soles.

Find a good tote or backpack to keep your tennis items organized and ready for the court.

TENNIS

To Play

- O sports bra
- O tennis skirt or shorts
- O tennis shirt
- O tennis dress & under shorts
- O warm up pants
- O warm up jacket
- O socks and sneakers
- O visor or hat
- O headband
- O wristband
- O sunglasses or sports goggles

In The Bag

- O sweatpoof sunscreen & lip protection
- O racquet
- O water bottle
- O towel
- O pouch with wallet, phone & keys
- O cooling neckband

GOLF

For **Ladies Who Links**, there are endless possibilities for travel to play at some of the most spectacular locations in the world. Whether you are just starting out, or a scratch golfer, when packing for a **Golf Holiday**, we like a layered approach. Look for pieces that have some stretch for comfort and style. There are many fantastic looking sportswear styles that are perfect for your day on the greens. Start with a smart looking **sport shirt**, well fitting, **shorts, slacks or skirt**, and add a **belt** for a neat, tucked in look. **Golf shoes** with support are important, and designs have come a long way in the last few years providing some chic styles that can put you on the right fairway footing. Layer as needed, depending on the weather. There are many pockets in your golf bag that can be utilized for stashing essentials. Have a system for storage so you know where everything is in case of the unexpected, like a sudden thunderstorm.

In the evening, most resorts are **Casually Chic**. A **wrap dress** with **sandals** or **wedges**, or a pair of **slacks,** and a **top**, should cover the majority of the places you will visit. **When in doubt, send us an email and, as always, we will do the research.**

J. McLaughlin's Catalina Fabric top is our favorite for fit and style. Pair with shorts or skirt with a bit of stretch, to go from the 1st Tee to the 19th Hole in fashion.

GOLF

ON THE COURSE
- O sports bra
- O sport shirt: sleeveless, short or long sleeved
- O shorts, pants or skirt
- O belt
- O sweater or polar fleece layer
- O lightweight vest
- O golf shoes & socks
- O sunglasses
- O hat, cap or visor
- O golf gloves

IN THE BAG
- O pouch with wallet, cell phone, keys
- O tees, repair tool, ball marker
- O balls: at least 6
- O waterproof jacket & pants
- O sunscreen & lip protection
- O towel
- O water bottle
- O snack
- O clubs
- O uv protective umbrella

CHAPTER 5
WEDDINGS

Destination Weddings

Day Weddings

Evening Weddings

Rehearsal Dinner

Lunches and Brunches

Top 10 Wedding Guest Tips

DESTINATION WEDDINGS

We receive so many emails from our readers asking us for help in navigating their wardrobe choices for Destination Weddings. When deciding what to pack, your choices should take into consideration **the destination, the weather,** and **the scale of the events.**

It seems like all weddings qualify as **destination weddings** these days, even if they are in your own town. No longer single service invitations, nuptials have been transformed into weekends of celebration; **the rehearsal dinner, wedding lunch, wedding, reception,** and **brunch on Sunday.** so it is important to plan ahead. While many weddings take place in tropical settings, there are endless locations both home and abroad that will require several different looks. If you are unsure, ask the bride or her family what is appropriate. You can also **send us a message and we will do the research** and give you the scoop.

Our packing list for **Destination Weddings** is based on a three to four day stay and assumes attendance at the rehearsal dinner, wedding, and a bridal lunch or brunch.

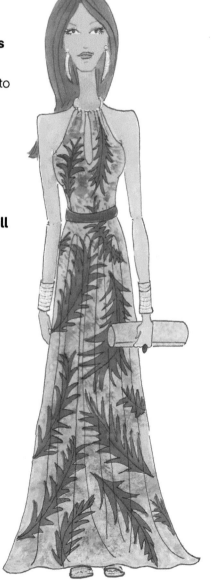

Non-stop fun can take its toll so treat yourself to a little pampering. Book your hair, nails, or massage in advance of your trip. Appointments fill up quickly.

DAY

- ○ 1 top
- ○ 2 day dresses
- ○ 1 cardigan sweater
- ○ 1 pair of jeans: denim, white or black
- ○ 1 light jacket or blazer: optional

EVENING

- ○ 1 evening top
- ○ 1 pair of pants
- ○ 1 cocktail dress
- ○ 1 festive dress
- ○ 1 evening dress if formal attire

SHOES

- ○ 1 pair of comfortable shoes for walking
- ○ 1 pair of medium heeled or wedges
- ○ 1 pair of evening shoes or sandals

ACCESSORIES

- ○ 1 or 2 scarves or pashminas
- ○ 1 belt
- ○ 1 tote for day
- ○ 1 clutch for evening
- ○ jewelry
- ○ any sports gear you may need

Day Weddings

All you need is love . . . And a smashing ensemble to celebrate the happy occasion. In deciding what to wear, your choice should echo the **mood of the wedding** and reflect the **time of day**. Avoid white, or shades close to white. Red can also be a no-no; remember, this is the bride's special day, so don't try to steal the spotlight. And never wear black, except in the evening when the wedding may be **Black Tie**. In any case, you might want to check with the family or ask the bride, or ask us for **specific advice to be sure**. Many of the old standards simply do not apply in attending today's modern ceremonies.

For a **morning or lunchtime ceremony**, we recommend a **silk dress, pumps, a small shoulder bag, and daytime jewelry. Hats and fascinators** are optional, but ever-so-stylish, especially since the royal wedding of **Kate and William,** the **Duke and Duchess of Cambridge**. And **gloves**, which were at one time *de rigueur*, have become an exception rather than a fashionable norm, but can look rather chic.

You can generally plan on other activities to go along with the wedding's festivities. Use one of our blank "Event and Packing Lists" in the back of the book.

Evening Weddings

The general rule of thumb is **the later the wedding and reception, the dressier your outfit should be.** As the nuptials move to the afternoon, with a dinner following, the attire becomes more along the lines of **evening wear.** We love to be **festive** in something that has a bit of shimmer, like **satin, silk, or brocade. Sequins and jeweled details** can also be quite celebratory. But don't go too far with the sparkle, remember: the bride should be the star of the show.

Traditionally, a wedding at **5 p.m. or later is considered to be Black Tie Formal.** For this, we suggest a **long or short formal dress, party shoes,** or **sandals, sparkling jewelry** and a **beautiful evening clutch.** We look for a **rich fabric and shades** that can glimmer in the candlelight and still look terrific through hours of celebration. When the invitation reads **"Black Tie Optional,"** we would suggest a **short festive dress,** unless all your friends are opting for long. Again, please ask us and we will do the research. Either way, you will look spectacular.

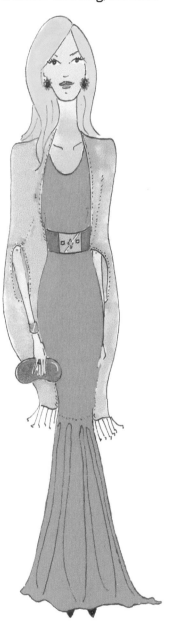

When attending a wedding in a church or synagogue, remember to dress respectfully, covering your bare arms and neckline with a wrap or jacket.

REHEARSAL DINNER AND LUNCHES

In general, for the **Rehearsal Dinner, a cocktail dress** and **pumps** is the right attire, unless it is a themed event, like a **Western Hoe Down** or a **Tropical Luau**. Take a **wrap** for warmth and a **clutch** to hold your essentials. Since it is the rehearsal and not the wedding, it is perfectly acceptable to wear a **Little Black Dress, LBD**, especially in colder climates. And why not? It is always appropriate and ever so chic.

Lunches and Brunches are **less formal**, depending on the venue. At a **club or a restaurant**, you can never go wrong with a **wrap dress, simple jewelry** and **wedges or heels**. If the event is more casual, such as a picnic: jeans, a blouse and flats or wedges will do nicely. If on the beach or a boat, we pair a bathing suit with a fabulous tunic.

Heels?
How high?
Find the heel height
that works for you
and that you can
wear comfortably
for hours. Say "NO"
to sore feet.

We like
to buy shoes
1/2 size larger, then
slip in a gel bed for
great comfort and
fit. Never travel
with new shoes.

TOP 10 WEDDING GUEST TIPS

Tip 1. DO RSVP promptly! The family will appreciate it.

Tip 2. DON'T procrastinate in **sending a gift**. Find out where the bride is registered and pick one that fits your budget and taste. When in doubt, a silver or silver plated picture frame, engraved with the wedding date is always appropriate and appreciated.

Tip 3. If you are unclear on the dress code, especially if there is a theme or destination involved, it is perfectly acceptable to ask the bride or her parents on the preferred style. **Or DO write to us and let us do the research!**

Tip 4. It is generally acknowledged that **black is not worn** unless the wedding is after 5:00 pm or formal. So **DON'T**, unless you want to buck the system. Better to break a rule when you know a rule.

Tip 5. Ditto on wearing white – **DON'T**, unless the bride requests.

Tip 6. DO be on time to the ceremony. It is not good form to follow the bride down the aisle unless you are holding her train, and you are not Pippa Middleton, darling.

Tip 7. DON'T duck the receiving line to get to the bar. Give a warm, but brief, well wish. This is not the time for a lengthy conversation.

Tip 8. Speaking of the bar – have fun, but **DON'T** overdo it. And if you are not expected to toast – please **DON'T.**

Tip 9. DON'T complain about the food. Actually, **DON'T complain about ANYTHING!**

Tip 10. DO write a thank you note soon after the party. If it is a close friend, call as well. **DO** exclaim profusely at the fabulosity of it all! **"Best Wedding Ever!"**

Chapter 6
Sports and Adventure

Ski and Après-Ski

Safari

Dude Ranch

Hiking

Biking

Water Sports

Spas

SKI

Look effortlessly chic when you hit the slopes this ski season by upgrading your schussing with stylish **ski wear**. Even if you are not a skier, your days on holiday will be spent in glorious outdoor activities such as **cross country skiing** and **snowshoeing,** among others.

When thinking of what to wear, nothing looks better than a **fitted jacket, preferably hip length or slightly longer,** paired with comfortable yet **slim ski pants**. While there are many excessively expensive brands available, you don't have to spend a fortune to look fabulous. The fit is key, so take your gear to a tailor for any tweaking you may need. **Helmets** are a must-have for slopeside safety. If you are renting your gear, it is a good idea to bring your own helmet. You can pack it efficiently in your bag by filling it with **socks** and other **small items**.

Packing for skiing can be a challenge with the bulky winter clothing. We generally use a **large rolling duffle** for all of our ski things and heavy items, and take a **smaller carry on size** for our après-ski fashion. Invest in a good pair of ski boots that are well fitted. In general, resorts will have an excellent selection of skis and poles to rent.

Tuck into your pockets: credit card, cash, lipstick/chapstick, tissues, phone and mints. Always use the same pockets so you can find things with frosty fingers.

SKI | PACKING LIST

DAYWEAR

- O 2 pairs of long underwear
- O 1 or 2 ski pants
- O 1 or 2 ski jackets
- O 1 zip-neck polar fleece or wool sweater
- O 1 polar fleece vest

ACCESSORIES & BOOTS

- O 1 tote bag or boot bag
- O sunglasses
- O 2 pairs of ski socks
- O 1 ski hat
- O 1 headband
- O 1 neck gator
- O 1 pair of leg gators for powder skiing
- O 1 pair of ski gloves
- O 1 pair of sunglasses
- O 1 pair of snow boots
- O hand & feet warmers

GEAR

- O 1 ski helmet
- O 1 pair of goggles
- O 1 pair of ski poles
- O 1 pair of skis
- O 1 pair of ski boots

APRÈS — SKI

Once you have your slope side attire set, you will want to pack for the essential **Après-Ski**, defined as the end of the ski day when one heads off for some hot drinks, a cold beer, wine, or champagne – divine! Generally there is a break between après-ski and dinner. This is the time set aside for naps, massages, catching up on emails and such.

In the **States**, the great resorts all have an iconic **western atmosphere** that lends itself to casual cowgirl wear, **leather** and **suede**. **Europe** is known for its **alpine vibe** with **Nordic sweaters** and crisp **piped-wool jackets**. If you are heading to a **laidback resort** like **Steamboat** or **Stratton**, the après-ski look and the evening attire can be very similar.

For evening wear in the tonier resorts such as **Aspen, St. Moritz**, or **Gstaad**, you will want to step it up with some **suede**, **fur**, and pack a **cocktail dress**. We suggest packing some **statement jewelry** for added nighttime glamour.

To Apres-Ski in style anywhere, you cannot go wrong with jeans, a cozy turtleneck sweater, boots and a fur or faux fur vest.

Après – Ski | packing list

Après-Ski & Evenings In Casual Resorts

- ○ 3 sweaters
- ○ 3 pairs of jeans: denim, suede or leather
- ○ 1 vest: down, suede or fur

Evenings In More Formal Resorts

- ○ 1 cocktail dress
- ○ 2 evening pants
- ○ 3 evening tops
- ○ 1 pair of pumps
- ○ statement jewelry

Shoes

- ○ 1 pair of low heeled or wedge boots
- ○ 1 pair of high-heeled boots

Accessories

- ○ 1 clutch
- ○ 1 belt
- ○ jewelry
- ○ 1 or 2 cashmere scarves or wraps
- ○ gloves
- ○ shearling or fur jacket and hat: optional

SAFARI

Take a walk on the wild side! A safari is truly an unforgettable experience – some say life changing – and we agree. Intimately witnessing the earth and animal kingdom come to life is both fascinating and mezmerizing. You will want to spend as much time as you can out on the prowl, and what to wear is key to your comfort and well-being. The temperature can be quite chilly before dawn, and after sunset, then very hot midday, so **dress in layers** for the broad range of temperatures.

Safari apparel is based around the colors of the landscape; **khaki, neutrals and greens**. But before you go shopping, look in your closet for your favorite **khakis** and **shirts** – we like the **chic mix and match look** rather than the all out "Safari Suit."

In the **evening**, dress casual: **slacks, jeans, blouses, and tunics** and don't forget your **wrap** or **jacket**. For **sightseeing**, we suggest a **simple dress** and **cardigan**. A good looking **tote** is also key, for holding onto your **extra layers, camera, trip journal,** and the like.

Watch your weight! Many safaris involve travel on small planes and your bag is closely monitored. Contact your outfitter for guidelines.

SAFARI | PACKING LIST

DAYWEAR

- ○ 2 camisoles
- ○ 3 cotton tops
- ○ 1 khaki shirt
- ○ 1 pair of shorts
- ○ 1 pair of khaki pants
- ○ 1 pair of jeans
- ○ 1 sweater
- ○ 1 vest
- ○ 1 jacket

EVENING WEAR

- ○ 2 tops or tunics
- ○ 1 casual dress
- ○ 1 pair of pants or jeans
- ○ 1 cardigan

SHOES

- ○ 1 pair of comfortable walking shoes or boots
- ○ 1 pair of sandals or flip-flops
- ○ 1 pair of wedges for evening

ACCESSORIES

- ○ sunglasses
- ○ 1 tote bag
- ○ 1 belt
- ○ 1 pair of leather gloves
- ○ 1 or 2 pashmina or wraps
- ○ 1 hat
- ○ 1 pair binoculars
- ○ 1 safari journal
- ○ camera and lenses

DUDE RANCH

Howdy Partner! Wondering what to wear on a **western riding** trip? You're in the great tradition of the rugged cowboys of the Wild West, your seat is deep in the saddle, and your horse is ready to go. Why not have some fun and dress the part! Good **jeans** are a must, as are **cowboy boots**; but after that, it is up to you. Try a **western shirt**, a great **fringed jacket** and of course, a **handsome western hat**.

With wholesome activities, like **trail rides, fishing, swimming, and shooting** going on from morning to night, a cowgirl has got to get in gear.

The temperature can be quite chilly in the morning, beautifully warm during the day, and even a bit nippy at night. We suggest a selection of **layering pieces** that will have you trotting on your way. By **day, a tank or tee shirt under a long sleeve shirt**, topped with a **vest** or **jacket**. Nightfall brings cozy dinners around the camp fire and we dress up with a bit of **suede, leather and gussied-up western wear** to keep you in great style sunrise to sunset.

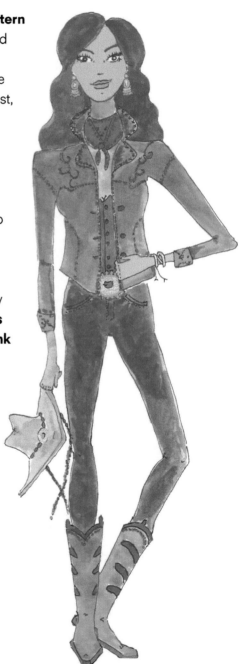

If you are planning on fishing, or other active pursuits check with the ranch to see what gear is available. They may have everything you need.

Dude Ranch | PACKING LIST

Daywear

- O 3 tanks or t-shirts
- O 2 long sleeved shirts
- O 2 pairs of jeans
- O 1 pair of spandex shorts to wear under jeans
- O 1 sweater
- O 1 vest
- O 1 waterproof jacket

Evening Wear

- O 3 evening tops
- O 1 pair of jeans
- O 1 suede skirt or jean skirt
- O 1 jacket: jean, suede or leather
- O 1 poncho or wrap

Shoes

- O 1 pair of western boots for riding
- O 1 pair of comfortable walking shoes
- O 1 pair of tevas or flip-flops
- O 1 pair of knee high boots

Accessories

- O 1 bandana or scarf
- O 1 belt
- O 1 pair of gloves
- O 1 hat
- O western jewelry

HIKING

Whether you are hiking for an hour, a day, or a week, you will be comfortable in the right gear if you **dress in layers**. Weather can range from chilly mornings to scorching afternoons, and levels of intensity can vary within a short period of time so it is important to be prepared. Wear what is comfortable for the season and time of day, then stash your extra layers in your pack.

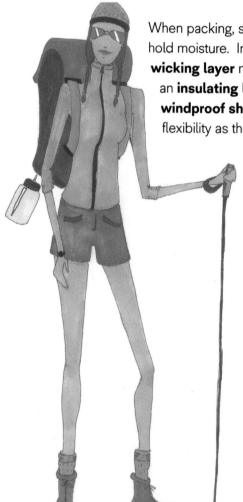

When packing, stay away from cotton clothing, which tends to hold moisture. Instead, you will want to start with a **lightweight wicking layer** next to your skin, then, depending on the climate, an **insulating layer** and then top off with a **waterproof and windproof shell**. An unlined **nylon jacket** will allow greater flexibility as the temperature varies. **Long pants that transform into shorts** are a good idea. Alternatively, you can wear lycra shorts under your hiking pants.

For **evenings**, the attire depends on your destination. If camping in tents or cabins, activewear will do the trick in most cases. If you are stopping at inns, or hotels, a pair of black pants, knit top, wrap, and wedges can work very nicely. Let us know where you are going and we will have some stylish suggestions. See Page 86 **Combination Travel**.

Boots should be waterproof and comfortable, with good traction and support. High or low cut is up to you but never take a new pair of boots on a hike.

Hiking | PACKING LIST

Sportswear
- ○ 2 sports bras
- ○ 3 wicking shirts: sleeveless or t-shirt
- ○ 2 pairs of pants & shorts or zips
- ○ 1 polar fleece top
- ○ 1 neck gator or bandana
- ○ 1 lightweight vest

For Cooler Weather
- ○ 1 pair of long underwear
- ○ 1 pair of gloves
- ○ 1 warm hat
- ○ hand and feet warmers
- ○ 1 down vest and jacket

Shoes And Gear
- ○ 1 pair of hiking boots
- ○ 1 pair of hiking poles
- ○ 1 miner's head lamp
- ○ 1 pair of leg gators
- ○ 1 pair of comfortable shoes

In The Backpack
- ○ identification, money, credit card
- ○ water bottle
- ○ cell phone and camera in waterproof bag
- ○ sunglasses with IREX rating of 100
- ○ 1 hat: brimmed or baseball
- ○ map or GPS
- ○ sunscreen & lip protection
- ○ sanitizing hand wipes
- ○ friction stick and blister pads
- ○ 1 waterproof and windproof jacket & pants
- ○ 1 waterproof pack cover

BIKING

Free wheeling on the open road! What an adventure! A holiday on wheels can provide a change of scenery and atmosphere. There are different kinds of **biking trips**. Some stop at **hotels, inns, and castles** along the way, with the organizer carting your luggage to the next stop-over, and you will need to **pack clothes for the evenings**. Other trips will be more **rugged; while camping out far from civilization**, the attire will be **casual** all the way.

In either case, biking requires **sleek and snug clothing** for great aerodynamics. Start with a supportive **sports bra** and a **sleeveless t-shirt**, add a **cycling jersey, vest and lightweight jacket** depending on the temperature. Wear **biking shorts or leggings, lightweight socks, and good biking shoes** or sneakers. Don't forget your **gloves, biking helmet, refillable water bottle,** and **sunglasses** as well.

For packing for evenings on a bike tour, we suggest **knit separates that don't wrinkle**, because your luggage will most likely be sent ahead of you and not unpacked until you arrive. A pair of stylish wedges and a fabulous pashmina will complete your look.

Wear brightly colored clothes for visibility to drivers. Have reflectors on your clothing and lights on your bike when riding at night.

BIKING | PACKING LIST

SPORTSWEAR

- O 2 sports bras
- O 2 wicking shirts: sleeveless or t-shirt
- O 2 cycling jerseys
- O 1 lightweight jacket
- O 2 pairs of biking shorts or leggings
- O 1 pair of arm and leg warmers

ACCESSORIES

- O 1 pair of biking shoes or sneakers
- O 1 pair of gloves
- O 1 biking helmet
- O 1 backpack or handlebar pack

IN THE BACKPACK OR HANDLEBAR PACK

- O water bottle
- O cell phone with GPS
- O sunglasses
- O camera
- O sunscreen & lip protection
- O lip balm
- O repair kit
- O snack bars or gels for energy
- O passport, identification, or driver's license
- O cash & credit card
- O 1 small first-aid kit
- O 1 waterproof pack cover
- O 1 waterproof top & bottom

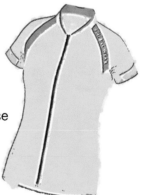

WATER SPORTS

Rafting, Paddling, Surfing, Longboarding

Whether standing up or sitting down, hitting the water is a wet and wild experience. Whatever your preferred water sport, here are some tips on dressing for comfort and safety. **Sun protection** is of the utmost priority when on the water. A nasty burn is going to damage your skin and ruin your holiday. so your first layer should be a waterproof, **broad spectrum sunscreen**. While naked, apply over your whole body, tip to toes. The next layer is a **bathing suit**, make sure it can withstand water pressure without flying off. Add a **UV Protective Rash Guard** or shirt and a pair of board shorts or quick drying shorts. If you are surfing or paddleboarding that is pretty much all you need.

For paddling and kayaking, add a **brimmed sun hat** with a cap strap to keep it clipped to your shirt. For cooler weather, you will want to add a **dry suit**, **paddling jacket** or **polar fleece**. And a life jacket is always a good idea.

When rafting the rapids, you will be required to wear a **helmet** and **life jacket** for safety. A waterproof paddle jacket is also a great piece to layer.

There are 6 classes of rapids from Easy to Extreme. Be aware of your level of expertise when choosing a rafting adventure.

WATER SPORTS | PACKING LIST

ON THE BOARDS

- O sunglasses & croakie
- O 2 bathing suits
- O 2 uva protective rash guards
- O 2 pairs of board shorts or fast drying nylons
- O 1 wet suit for cooler weather

PADDLING AND RAFTING

- O sunglasses & croakie
- O 2 bathing suits
- O 2 uva protective tops
- O 2 paddling or quick drying shorts
- O 1 paddle jacket
- O 1 hat with lid latch hat retainer
- O 1 pair of water shoes or strap on sandals
- O 1 life vest
- O 1 helmet

IN YOUR DRY BAG

- O water bottle
- O cell phone & camera in waterproof bag
- O sunscreen & lip protection
- O snacks
- O wax
- O towel
- O change of clothes

TO THE SPA

Ah Spaaaaaaa! The most delightful thing you can do for yourself is book a healthy holiday at a spa. Whether you go with friends, significant others or all by yourself, you will return **rejuvenated and refreshed**. Depending on your preference, be prepared to be pampered, scheduled into rigorous activities, or a bit of both. If you are wondering how to find the right spa for you, just drop us an email and we will help you select the one that suits your style. Your packing will reflect a variety of activities, so always **check the spa website** for specifics.

For daywear, for everything from **Aerobics to Zumba**, the rule of thumb is to dress in layers. Always have something cozy on hand to warm your muscles after the workout. With all of the chic active wear on the market, we are happy to report that the days of sweatpants are over. Why not look totally stylish when working out. If you will be hiking, please see our **Hiking Chapter** on what to pack.

Evenings at a Spa are meant for relaxing dinners, elective lectures and classes, and watching movies where the dress is casual comfort. In warm weather, white jeans, tunic and sandals, with a fun statement necklace or earrings. In colder weather, relax in a pair of comfortable stretch pants, knee high boots, and a sweater topped with a fur or faux fur vest.

TO THE SPA | PACKING LIST

DAYWEAR

- O 3 sports bras
- O 3 sleeveless or short sleeve athletic tops
- O 3 athletic bottoms: shorts, capris, or ankle
- O 2 long sleeve polar fleece or lightweight wool tops
- O 1 light down vest
- O 1 swimsuit, cap & goggles
- O 1 water & windproof jacket

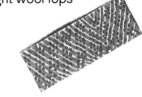

SHOES AND ACCESSORIES

- O 1 pair of exercise shoes
- O 1 pair of flip-flops
- O 1 hat
- O 1 water bottle
- O 1 day pack or tote
- O head band & wrist band

EVENINGS

- O 3 casual evening tops
- O 2 pairs of stretchy pants or jeans
- O 1 cardigan
- O 1 wrap or pashmina
- O 1 pair of wedges
- O 1 pair of boots for cooler weather
- O 1 fur, faux fur or down vest for cooler weather

COMBINATION TRAVEL

Combo travel involves packing for two or more venues and requires creative and thoughtful planning. You could be enjoying an outdoor adventure like **hiking** or **rafting** as part of a longer holiday, where you will be visiting towns and sightseeing. Or if your journey takes you **biking** on the road, stopping at castles and inns along the way, you will want something a little more elegant to wear than spandex. On top of all of the activity wear and gear to pack, you will need some outfits for "in-town" destinations. Our indomitable hiking friend, Stacy Morse, recommends packing your travel clothing in a large **Ziploc® Bag**, to keep it separated from your activity gear.

On many overnight adventure trips, you will leave your suitcase at a hotel, or with your organizer who will shuttle them to your next destination. In either case, your clothing will remain in your bag so it is really important to pack **non-wrinkling fabrics**. There are incredible wardrobe choices that fit in to this category, from tee shirts to evening gowns and everything in between. Stick to a **neutral color scheme** so that everything mixes and matches. Khaki, Black, White, and prints of similar shades will simplify your dressing choices. You can get much mileage from a brightly colored **wrap** and a few pieces of high-impact, light weight **statement jewelry**.

To get the air out of a Ziploc® bag, insert a straw into the corner, and zip. Then suck the air out through the straw until compressed.

COMBINATION TRAVEL | PACKING LIST

For an extended stay of 3 or 4 days, we recommend adding the following items to your bag. If staying longer, increase the number of tops and add another knit dress.

○ 1 wrap or knit dress
○ 1 pair of black or khaki stretch pants
○ 2 tops of a non-wrinkle fabric
○ 1 cardigan sweater
○ 1 pair of flats or sandals
○ 1 pair of wedges or heels
○ 1 medium size purse, like a crossbody bag
○ 1 packable sunhat
○ pashmina or wrap
○ statement jewelry
○ outerwear of appropriate warmth

Many people like to ship a bag to their destination. We prefer to pack well and travel with our belongings, especially when traveling out of the country.

CHAPTER 7
COUNTRY SPORT

Shooting
Clay Shooting | Upland Shooting | Formal Shooting

Fishing
Fly Fishing | Spin Reel

Equestrian Adventure

Clay Shooting

Clay Shooting is a great sport for women who love the outdoors where the targets, "clay pigeons", replicate the excitement of shooting in the wild landscape. It is one of the few sports where men and women compete on equal ground, toe to toe, as it were. Your apparel should reflect the palette found in nature: tans, browns, greens and muted shades. Layering is the key to comfort and style, depending on the temperature. Start with a pair of jeans or long pants, add a shirt, **shooting vest,** and low heeled boots. **Eye and ear protection** is mandatory, and a hat provides a safeguard against falling shot.

Safety first is the rule! Keep the shotgun pointed in a safe direction. Never point it at another person or anywhere you don't want to shoot. Always check to make sure the gun is not loaded and that there are no obstructions in the barrel. Keep the gun's safety lock on until just before you shoot. Never touch the trigger until you want to shoot. Store the gun safely in a locked cabinet.

There are many ways to shoot clays or clay pigeons. In each, the flight of the target mimics that of a bird or animal in nature. **Trap Shooting** launches targets from a single source. **Skeet Shooting** involves targets propelled from two or more stations while a **Sporting Clay Course** consists of a series of shooting stands, laid out in a pattern. Shooters rotate to each numbered station and take aim at moving targets thrown from a variety of launchers.

CLAY SHOOTING | PACKING LIST

CLAY SHOOTING

- O sport shirt
- O jeans or khaki pants
- O shooting vest
- O waterproof boots or shoes
- O ears plugs or headset
- O sunglasses or protective eyewear
- O hat or cap
- O waterproof jacket
- O shell bag
- O gun
- O gun bag

If you are just learning to shoot, contact Orvis or other reliable companies and organizations for authorized schools and lessons.

UPLAND SHOOTING

In Field or Upland Shooting, the hunter pursues upland birds such as pheasant, quail, woodcock, grouse and the like. These birds often live in the underbrush and gun dogs are used to locate and retrieve them. You will be in the thick of it, and your clothing choices should be well suited to the terrain and the weather.

Start with **brush pants and shirt,** made of a tightly woven fabric which resists snagging on bushes and prickers. Add an **orange vest** and **cap** for safety when shooting in the field. A pair of **snake boots** will keep you comfy and safe.

A **Recoil Shoulder Pad** can be used to protect your shoulder and lessen the "kick" from the gun. And many shirts and vests have a built in shoulder patch.

Safety first and always! Learn the safety rules of shooting to enhance your experience and that of your fellow shooters.

UPLAND SHOOTING | PACKING LIST

FIELD OR UPLAND SHOOTING

- O khaki shirt
- O brush pants
- O shooting vest
- O orange cap or hat
- O shooting gloves
- O waterproof jacket
- O ear plugs or headset
- O sunglasses or protective eyewear
- O waterproof boots
- O shell bag

FORMAL SHOOTING

For a shooting holiday in **Europe** or a **Continental Style** venue, the attire becomes more stylized and bespoke. You might wear **moleskin** or **tweed**, **pants** or **breeks**, socks, **garters**, and **waterproof boots**. On top you will need a tailored shirt, scarf, and vest, or a blazer. To top it all off, a waterproof wax cotton or heavier jacket and a **hat with a brim**, which comes in handy in case of rain.

A more formal style of shooting is likely to have **Cocktail** or even **Black Tie** attire for evenings. A classic look is black pants, a silk blouse, a lovely cashmere or fur wrap, and a bit of festive jewelry. If Black Tie is called for, you would wear an evening dress or separates. When in doubt let us know and **we will do the specific research** on your shooting lodge, manor house, castle, ranch or estancia.

For a beginner, our expert at Orvis recommends a lightweight 12 gauge with a 26" barrel with very little kickback or recoil.

FORMAL SHOOTING | PACKING LIST

EUROPEAN STYLE SHOOTING

- ○ dress shirt
- ○ pants or breeks
- ○ neck scarf
- ○ socks
- ○ garters
- ○ vest
- ○ jacket
- ○ waterproof top layer
- ○ hat
- ○ ear plugs or headset
- ○ sunglasses or protective eyewear
- ○ shooting gloves
- ○ shell bag

FLY FISHING

Face it, you're hooked! Humans have gone to the river for sustenance, and we suspect for fun, since the beginning of time. Fishing can be as simple as a string on a stick or as high-tech as the latest GPS fish finder.

Whether **wading streamside with a fly rod,** or **casting from shore** or a boat with a **spin reel**, a fishing holiday is a fantastic adventure in the great outdoors. Hopefully, your conditions will be perfect, but when you follow our packing list, you will have the right gear to weather any storm.

You could be going to **Alaska** for salmon, to the **Bahamas** for bonefish, or **Out West** for trout, but your basics will remain the same. Wear layers of breathable, comfortable pieces, and waterproof and sunproof outer gear all in shades of nature to blend with the elements . . . and so the fish can't see you coming!

Protect yourself from the sun. Make sure your sunglasses are polarized. Apply your UVA and UVB sunscreen and lip protection frequently.

Streamside

- camisole
- uv protective shirt
- quick drying shorts or pants
- waders
- non-slip waterproof boots
- fishing vest
- polarized sunglasses
- shade hat or cap
- waterproof jacket

On The Flats

- bathing suit
- light colored uv protective shirt
- quick drying pants
- face buff
- polarized sunglasses with croakie
- non slip flat boots
- neoprene wading socks
- waterproof jacket
- hat or visor
- fishing gloves

In The Waterproof Pack

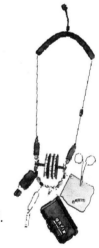

- sunscreen & lip protection
- water bottle
- snack
- waterproof bag with phone, cash, credit card & i.d.
- towel

Gear

- fly rod and reel
- fly box
- hooks, leaders, tippet, snips, wire cord zingers, magnifiers, flotant, forceps, strike indicators, sink putty, landing net

DEEP SEA FISHING

We love the excitement of steaming out to sea for a day of adventure on the open water. **Fishing is a universal pursuit** and wherever your travels take you, there will be enthusiastic partakers both for sport and sustenance.

When on the water, sun protection is critical. Never underestimate the power of the sun. When you are going out to sea or lake, or surf casting on the beach, the effect of the sun's reflection will be multiplied. Must haves start with a **high SPF**, water-proof sunscreen, then add a hat with a brim, a UV protective shirt and face buff. There are so many stylish choices in sun protection clothing available that you no longer have to look like you borrowed your dad's shirt. Our friends at **GlamourpussNYC** have a sensational selection. As in most outdoor activities, layers are the way to go. Always be prepared for a sudden shift in weather and temperature.

If you are going out with a captain or charter, most likely all of your equipment will be supplied, so make sure to inquire.

We recommend a catch and release method of fishing. Unless you are going to eat the fish, let it go back for another day and another exciting catch.

DEEP SEA FISHING | PACKING LIST

DEEP SEA FISHING

- O bathing suit
- O t-shirt or camisole
- O uv protective shirt
- O shorts or lightweight pants
- O polar fleece top
- O non-slip boat shoes or sandals
- O polarized sunglasses with croakie
- O sun hat or cap
- O uv face buff
- O waterproof jacket

TO CARRY

- O sunscreen & lip protection
- O water
- O towel
- O snack
- O waterproof bag with phone, cash, credit card & i.d.

GEAR

- O spin rod and reel
- O tackle box
- O hooks
- O lures
- O pliers
- O fish hook extractor
- O scale
- O line cutter
- O crimper
- O hook sharpener
- O swivels
- O sinkers
- O floats
- O net

EQUESTRIAN ADVENTURE

Seeing a country on horseback is a unique experience to go off the beaten path and to have an adventure of a lifetime. And whether you are new to the saddle or an experienced rider, you can find a holiday that is perfect for your equestrian level of experience. You can gallop on the **African plains**, rustle cattle in the **Wild West**, trot along the fine food and wine trail in the **Loire Valley**, enjoy an exhilarating canter in the **Spanish surf**, or from **Palace to Palace in Rajasthan,** and everything in between.

Depending on the trip location and type, you may have to transport belongings on a pack horse with a **strict weight policy.** On other jaunts, your luggage will be moved ahead for you, from place to place, and you will have a little more leeway with your packing. Consult your trip planner for the weight specifics or **contact us to do the research**.

Most equestrian pursuits, such as jumping, dressage, eventing, and polo have their own approved apparel, some of which is strictly enforced. Riding holidays have no such standards, but we like a neat, pulled together look of riding in the English saddle: a pair of jodhpurs, shirt, belt, boots, and vest or jacket. Your most important piece of equipment is your **helmet or hard hat**, which is critical to protect against head injuries. Make sure yours meets the **ASTM/SEI** standards for safety. If you are going on a **western trek**, we suggest checking out our **Dude Ranch Packing List** on Page 77.

Equestrian Adventure | PACKING LIST

In The Saddle

- O 1 riding helmet
- O 2 pairs of jodhpurs or jeans
- O 2 camisoles
- O 3 long sleeve shirts
- O 1 pair of spurs if needed
- O 1 protective or impact inflatable vest
- O 1 sweater or fleece
- O 1 lightweight vest
- O 1 belt
- O 1 pair of riding gloves
- O 1 pair of riding boots
- O 1 pair of paddock boots
- O 1 pair of half-chaps
- O 1 pair protective eyewear or sunglasses
- O 1 crop

In Your Pack

- O water
- O sunscreen & lip protection
- O snack
- O 1 pair of waterproof pants & jacket
- O 1 pair of flip flops
- O 1 pair of spare socks

Evenings

- O 3 evening tops
- O 2 pairs of slacks
- O 1 knit dress
- O 1 pair of wedges or boots
- O 1 cardigan
- O 1 wrap or pashmina

CHAPTER 8
FASHION ADVICE

---

10 Top Tips on Dressing

All About Dresses

Dressing for Your Body Type

How to Shop Online

10 Top Tips for Dressing

TIP # 1. Quality Trumps Quantity. Buy the best quality you can afford. Don't chase sales when you are likely to buy items because they are "a good deal." Of course, if there is a brand that you know and love that goes on sale, by all means **shop away!**

TIP # 2. Hunt for Wardrobe Holes. Go through your closet around the first of each

month and **put together your outfits for the next 30 days.** Identify what items are missing to complete your looks. We prefer monthly to seasonal dressing. June is totally different than August though they are both summer months. Ditto for December and February in winter, and in general, for the rest of the seasons.

TIP # 3. Timeless Not Trendy. Avoid fads and stick to the classics. They are your best investment in style. If you must have the "flavor of the month," don't invest heavily in it.

TIP # 4. Fit Is Everything. Find a good tailor, as most clothing needs a little tweak to fit best. Figure the cost of alterations into the purchase price of the item. Tip your tailor well.

TIP # 5. Don't Forget a Bit of TLC. Take care of your clothes. Follow instructions for laundry and dry cleaning. Go through your clothing for loose buttons or downed hems and fix them or have them fixed. Your wardrobe is an investment and time spent on maintenance will pay great dividends.

TIP # 6. Best Footwear Forward. Don't skimp on shoes. Cheap shoes look cheap. And do splurge on a good shoe brush, shoe polish, and everything you need for a quick do-it-yourself shine. Find a shoe repair shop to keep heels and soles looking good.

10 Top Tips for Dressing

TIP # 7. A Little Goes A Long Way. Don't wear short, tight, and low cut at the same time. It is much more alluring to pick one of your attributes to feature. If you have great legs, go with something short; if you have a toned shape, go with something fitted; if you have a lovely decollete, by all means, lower the neckline.

TIP # 8. Bigger May Be Better. If you think a dress is **too tight or too short – it is!** It is better to buy one size up, especially in knits, and have it tailored for the perfect fit.

TIP # 9. Keep Calm and Press On. Invest in a **Pants Presser** and use it as soon as you remove your pants or skirts. It will allow you multiple wearings without dry cleaning. If there is a spot, brush or wipe it off with a damp cloth before you use the presser.

TIP # 10. A Foundation for Fabulous. For clothes to look their best, invest in **undergarments and shapewear**. Don't forget the often-overlooked slip, which can create a smooth line without feeling tight.

How short is too short? This is a subjective measurement depending on your age, your body type and your personality. In recent years, women have turned up their hems a bit for a more youthful silhouette. Our best length is just above the knee.

ALL ABOUT DRESSES

WHY WEAR A DRESS?? Because we can, of course! There is nothing as easy and chic as the **"zip and go"** of putting on a dress. A good dress can take you from morning 'til night in style . . . **But which dress for where?**

DAY DRESSES This is the ultimate versatile wardrobe item. Put one on and you can go anywhere with confidence. There are broad ranges of fabric, color and pattern choices but all should be comfortable and stylish.

SUN DRESSES are usually **lightweight cotton or linen**. It is often a sleeveless shift, strapless, or A-line. Wear in warm climates with sandals, bangles and hoop earrings.

The **SHIRTDRESS** is a tried and true classic for shopping, around town or running off to meet a friend for lunch. Little **pumps** and a **smart bag or tote** complete the look.

A **WRAP DRESS** is THE go-to dress. The iconic brain child of designer **Diane von Furstenberg** is easy to wear and super great for travel. There are many other versions but the original is still the greatest.

A **SHEATH DRESS** is an universally complimentary style with a form fitting, but not too tight silhouette. Paired with a cardigan, and a "lady bag" it creates a timeless look. We love a well-fitting sheath for workplace **luncheons** and **charity events**.

COCKTAIL DRESSES It is time to let your hair down! Can be a little short or a little low cut – always worn with heels and a dash of sauce. For a great **Cocktail Dress**, choose fabrics that fit the season, like wool blends in the chilly climates and cotton and linen blends in the warmer ones. Silk is a wonderful four season fabric, as are some of the synthetics and knits.

LITTLE BLACK DRESS LBD is the go-to for evening attire. It says, "Let's party" in the most expedient way. There are many variations on this theme popularized by Holly Golightly in **Breakfast at Tiffany's**. Add high heel pumps, a clutch bag, and some gold and pearl jewelry and you are ready to go.

ALL ABOUT DRESSES

BUSINESS ATTIRE

For an event calling for **Business Attire**, we would suggest classic colors of black, navy blue, grey or another rich dark shade. And for **Business Events**, don't wear anything too short, low cut or tight. Pick a **Cocktail Dress** that is flattering and stylish and then add some punch with your accessories – a statement necklace and a brightly colored clutch can get you noticed.

FESTIVE DRESSING

A popular way of dressing, although few seem to know what the phrase means! We like to imagine **Cocktail Attire with a flash of bling**. Brocades, taffeta, metallic fabrics all add to the special occasion dress, so perfect for **Evening Weddings**, **Bar and Bat Mitzvahs** and Holiday Occasions. Metallic **sandals** and **clutch** complete the look.

BLACK TIE FORMAL

Ah, there is a lovely bit of glamour to a **Black Tie or Formal Event**. The question often asked of us is, **Long or Short?** If the event is a **Gala** or a **Ball** then a long dress is generally worn. If the event is on a week night, with an early start time and women coming directly from work, short dresses may be preferred. But there are many exceptions, so when in doubt, **ask your friends or ask us**. We will do the research and get back to you. In general, we would rather be in the minority wearing short, than long. But whichever you chose, wear an elegant jacket or wrap, a pair of evening sandals or pumps, carry a sparkling clutch, and your best jewelry.

WHITE TIE

Cinderella darling, it is time for the ball! **White Tie** requires the most formal, full-length gown with long gloves. You will want to bring a wrap or stole to cover your shoulders and carry a small jeweled clutch. To increase your sparkle, break out your real jewels or the good fakes. **Thumbs up to gloves!** At State Dinners, Debutante Balls and other very formal events, we suggest an **Opera Length** or **16 Button Glove** with a strapless or sleeveless gown. Wear the gloves for cocktails and the receiving line if there is one, then take them off when you arrive at the table for dinner.

How to Dress for your Body Type

Long And Lean: Thin and in proportion with a long slender shape

Hourglass: Curvy on top and bottom with a smaller waist

Apple Shape: Fuller on top and middle and slimmer on the bottom

Succulent Pears: If your lower body is larger than your upper body

Pretty Petite: Generally small all over

Lucky Long And Lean

Lucky you! This shape is every designer's muse. **You are thin and in proportion with a slender shape**. It is a very chic shape and most clothing will look good on you. But it doesn't mean that you can't look feminine. For a bit of a more curvy look, choose clothing that accentuates your bust line. **A peplum** can also add extra shape to your lower half and is so flattering.

Time For The Hourglass Figures

Curvy on top and bottom, with a smaller waist? You have a shapely HOURGLASS figure. Your curves are your best feature, so by all means play them up with dresses that keep your body in proportion while accentuating your small waist. You may want to wear a belt for added emphasis. While this is a **naturally sexy shape**, you should take care not to overplay the curves by going too tight. Especially with knits, we recommend buying one size up and having the midsection taken in to ensure a flawless fit all over.

Delicious Apple

Are you fuller on top and in the midsection and slimmer on the bottom? We call this a delicious APPLE SHAPE. You will want to choose necklines that are a little lower cut to emphasize your lovely bosom and take the attention off of your mid section. **Wear dresses** rather than separates for a pulled together look that will flatter your best features. Go a little shorter to show off your great legs.

HOW TO DRESS FOR YOUR BODY TYPE

SUCCULENT PEARS

If your lower body is larger than your upper body – join the club – this is the most common body type, and it is a juicy **PEAR SHAPE**. A **Fit and Flare** shape dress can be your best friend as the shape naturally flares just at the right spot to enhance your figure. And to draw the eyes upward, create some interest in the neckline with a statement necklace.

PRETTY PETITE

If you are small all over, we call this **PETITE.** You can wear most anything as long as it doesn't overwhelm your small size. A shorter length will make you appear taller. Your best style is simple and chic. We like **short sheaths** which will **flatter your shape.**

Illustration inspired by Project Gravitas

STEP BY STEP ONLINE SHOPPING

So now that you know how to pack for travel, here's some tips to help you shop for everything you need. If you are like most of today's busy women, working outside or inside the home, time is a precious commodity that is in all too short supply. In-store shopping is becoming more of a luxury, at the same time on-line shopping continues to grow at an exponential pace. With years of expertise, here is our best advice to maximize your time spent shopping online.

STEP 1. MEASURE UP!

MICHAEL KORS

Before you start, identify your body type and the style that suits you best.

It is important to accurately measure your body. Always keep the tape measure parallel to the floor and do not measure over clothing. The **Bust** should be measured around the fullest part and around your back. For **Sleeves**, measure from the top of shoulder to the cuff. Bend on one side to find the natural crease of your **Waist** and measure around the slimmest point above your navel and below your ribs. The **Rise** is the measure from the top of the item's waistband to the crotch. The **Inseam** measure is from the very top of the inside of your leg to the ankle. For **Hips**, stand with feet together, measure around the fullest part of hips and around your **Rear**.

glamourpuss NYC

STEP 2. SHOP WHAT YOU KNOW

Shop at department stores and with **designers that you know** and like, with quality and sizing that you can count on to be consistent.

STEP 3. SEARCH FOR IT!

TORY BURCH

The **Search Function** on sites is very helpful. If you are looking for something specific, like "black slacks" you can type it into the **Search Box** and options will appear. Clicking on the **Categories** will expand the list so you can find the items that interest you. The **Sort Function** is incredibly helpful as well. It lets you look through the pages by price, by style, by designer and by color. You can also sort by **Price** to find your price range. If you are just "window shopping," retail sites have a **"What's New"** or **"Current Trends"** that offer extensive editorial and fashion advice to makes it a pleasurable and informative experience, like reading a magazine. Also highly recommended is the **Sale** function which makes it so handy to spot great bargains without the fuss of rummaging through picked-over racks of clothing.

STEP BY STEP ONLINE SHOPPING

STEP 4. EUREKA! I'VE FOUND IT!

Once you have found an item that interests you, take the time to look at it using all of the information at your fingertips like **size charts, comments from other buyers, fabric content**, and so on.

BERGDORF GOODMAN

STEP 5. WILL THE SHOE FIT?

Use the **Fit Guides** for how something is sized. Keep a measuring tape in a drawer by your computer – just how short is a 19" skirt and where will it fall on me? Use the **Zoom** function and move it up and down on the image – it will tell you a lot about the color, pattern, texture and decorative details. Most sites now have **Video** capabilities that give you a visual on how the item moves on a body.

J.CREW

STEP 6. BUT, WILL IT FIT?

After consulting the size chart, if you are still in doubt about sizes, **order two sizes** and pick the one that fits you best. When ordering knits, you may want to go up one size so it is not too clingy, but that is a matter of fit preference. Remember that most purchases need **a trip to the tailor** for minor alterations. Find someone locally with good turn-around time and build it into the price of the garment. **Fit is everything!**

STEP 7. MORE IS MORE!

Since it is likely that you will be returning at least one item, take time to **explore the site for other purchases** that you may need – hosiery, shoes, purse, wrap, scarves, jewelry for your outfit or how about workout clothing, or rainy day gear?

STEP 8. SPEED DELIVERY

When it comes to shipping, if you can afford it, have your order expedited for **one or two day shipping time**, building the cost into the price of the garments. Then follow the **Check Out** instructions. You will receive an **Order Confirmation** by e-mail to print. Often if you spend over a certain amount, expedited shipping is free.

Nicole Miller

NET-A-PORTER

RALPH LAUREN

HOW TO SHOP ONLINE

STEP 9. THE FUN PART!

One of the absolute **advantages** of shopping online is when the package arrives. Instead of being crammed into a dressing room with bad lighting and a strange salesperson trying to be your friend, **you can sneak away to the privacy of your closet, trying your items on with your own shoes, jewelry, undergarments, and accessories.** You are able to assess whether this is a good piece for you and if you have the right accessories for it. You will know right away what is working for you so **keep a pen and packing slip handy to mark what is going back.** Fold the returns and place them back in the packaging right away.

STEP 10. SAYING GOODBYE!

Think of returning as just another step in the process, not a complicated chore. The retail shops have made returning a quick and easy task. Go to their website and **follow the instructions to print a return shipping label.** Each retailer is slightly different but all make the directions simple to follow. **Be considerate of the retailers**, and send off your returns right away. In many cases, you are not charged for the returns and you can leave the box on your doorstep for a courier.

CHAPTER 9
RESOURCES

Travel Safety

Where to Shop

Customized Packing Lists

TRAVEL SAFETY

When we talk about **Travel Safety**, there are a few steps to take to insure that your travels are as smooth as possible, and that you arrive feeling good and ready to go.

SECURITY

Be aware of any travel alerts and warnings for your destination. Contact the State Department http://www.state.gov/travel for the latest announcements.

Know what the **Identification Requirements** are for your destination. Contact the State Department by visiting: http://travel.state.gov/content/visas/english/general/americans-traveling-abroad.html

Check your Passport to make sure you have a least 6 months left until the expiration date. Some countries will not accept a Passport that is close to expiration.

Travel Documents should include Passport ID page, Foreign Visa, Itinerary, Hotel Confirmation, Airline Ticket, Driver's License, and Credit Cards.

Copy your documents electronically and on paper. Send a copy to your family or friends and save a version on your phone.

Research your destination to know about **local customs and laws** and then abide by them.

Have the contact information for the nearest **US Embassy** or **Consulate** at your destination. Go to http://www.usembassy.gov for a listing.

MONEY

Familiarize yourself with the **currency of the destination**, and plan on changing some money at the airport or your local bank before you go.

Travel with a back up **Credit Card**. Some people feel secure buying some **Travelers Checks** because they can be refunded easily if lost or stolen. But with the advancement of **Credit Card** and **ATM** technology, it may not be necessary in all but the most remote destinations.

Call your **Credit Card Company** and **Bank** to let them know you will be traveling, to avoid suspected fraud.

TRAVEL HEALTH

BEFORE YOU GO
Contact the **Center for Disease Control** for a list of recommended inoculations for your location. wwwnc.cdc.gov/travel/destinations/list

Determine whether your **Medical Insurance** will cover you when traveling and then consider buying travel insurance.

Pack your medications in your carry on bag. Bring back up prescriptions from your doctor and pack these in a safe place, not with the medication. Boost your defenses by taking Vitamin C before and during travel.

ON THE PLANE
Use **saline spray** or a dab of **Neosporin** in your nostrils, before and after the flight to keep your membranes moist and more resistant to infection. Since many germs are found on and around your seat, tuck a few **antibacterial wipes** into your bag and wipe down your seat, armrest and most importantly your tray table before you take your seat.

Don't touch any unnecessary surfaces, like other seats on the way to the lavatory. Bring an **antibacterial wipe** to the loo to open the door and to wipe other surfaces you will contact. Wipe your hands again when returning to your seat.

When in your seat, always have your **seatbelt fastened,** whether or not the seatbelt indicator is on. Turbulence often arrives unexpectedly.

Keep your air vent pointed just in front of your face to keep the air and germs moving or take a **portable travel air purifier** which hangs around your neck.

Hydrate by drinking plenty of water. Bring an empty, reusable water bottle, then fill it once you pass through security.

Move around a bit. Even if you can't get out of your seat, you can keep your muscles active with a series of **isometrics**, flexing and stretching your arms and legs, and rolling your neck gently.

To avoid pulls and strains, be careful how you lift and carry your bags. Remember to **lift with your legs**, not with your back. If you cannot manage getting your luggage to the overhead, ask someone to help.

WHERE TO SHOP

We are sharing some of our best **Online Retail Sources**, chosen for selection, quality, and ease of returning. When you shop through our website **What2WearWhere.com**, a percentage of our commissions from sale will be donated to our **Charity of the Month**.

Alexis Bittar • Amazon • Asos • Athleta
Fairchild Baldwin Bags • Barneys New York
Beauty.com • Beretta • Bergdorf Goodman
Brics Luggage • British Sporting Arms • Blair Hussain
Bloomingdales • Cabela's • Calypso St. Barths
Creel Mack • Diane von Furstenberg • Drugstore.com
Elaine Turner • Eponymous NYC • GAP • GlamourpussNYC
Hartman Luggage • Holland and Holland • Hunter Boots
Jack Rogers • J.CREW • J. McLaughlin • JP Crickets
Joan Hornig Jewelry • Julie Vos Jewelry • LL Bean
Lord & Taylor • Lulu Lemon • Massey Outfitters
Michael Kors • Milly • Moosejaw • Net-A-Porter
Nicole Miller • Nike • Nina Griscom • Nordstrom • Orvis
Oscar de la Renta • Paragon Sports • Patagonia
Project Gravitas • Ralph Lauren • REI
Saks Fifth Avenue • Stuart Weitzman
Sweaty Betty • The Outnet • Tory Burch
Walker and Wade • Zappos

We gratefully acknowledge our Affiliate Retail Sites
for the use of images throughout the book.

Acknowledgments

When I began **What2WearWhere** five years ago, there were friends who lent their name, expertise and great style to the site, and for this I am forever grateful.

As **W2WW Style Editor**, **Hilary Dick** has been an invaluable inspiration and muse.

Each of our **W2WW Fashion Editors** provided her generous guidance.
Mary Darling
Vanessa Deserio
Jill Fairchild
Leslie Johnson
Kalliope Karella Rena
Kick Kennedy
Nicole Hanley Mellon
Simone Mailman

The lovely and talented **Lara Glaister** for her brilliant sketches that capture the adventurous spirit of our **W2WW Girl**.

And other friends who pitched in to help.

Debbie Bancroft, Georgina Bland, Peggy Bitler,
Anastasia Gayol Cintron, Barbara Crocker, Parker Gentry,
Jamee Gregory, Denise Herman, Melanie Seymour Holland,
Jane Hottensen, Jack Lynch, Tracey Mactaggart, Susan Meyer,
Stacey Morse, Sophie Pyle, Celeste Rault, Isabella Rodriguez,
Kristina Saljanin, Deborah Skelly, Kevin Smith, Pam Taylor, Deni Wandt

Papa Dick Klopp for his ongoing support.

My amazing children **Adam**, **Jake** and **Kell** for taking me places I never thought I would go.

Charissa Blouch and **Maureen Rooney** of **Rooney Design.**

The Author

Karen Klopp, or KK to her friends, is the founder of **What2WearWhere.com**, a luxury lifestyle brand and website, that helps today's busy women dress for all of life's events, sports, and travel. *"We take the guess work out of dressing, the legwork out of shopping and the panic out of packing."* She has contributed to Quest Magazine and Huffington Post, and has appeared on radio and Good Day New York, offering stylish and practical answers to the age old question, "What do I wear!?"

With a background as a writer, award-winning documentary film producer, life-long conservationist, traveler, board member, event chairman, wife, and mother of three, KK has experienced nearly every kind of event that a woman must prepare for in life. Now, she has taken her expertise along with the hundreds of questions she has received regarding packing for travel, and turned it into a compact, organized, and entertaining guide to simplify the process.

Karen spent the early years of her career as a freelance writer and filmmaker with a focus on conservation and wildlife. In 1991, **"Amazon Diary"** was nominated for an Academy Award in the Feature Short category. In 1989, KK co-founded, with Amy Hatkoff, **The Women's Group**, a support group dedicated to women and children living in New York City shelters. From that experience came the co-authored book, **"How to Save The Children,"** a guide for individuals seeking to get involved in the lives of "at risk" children. In the same spirit, a portion of the proceeds from this book, as well at the website, are **donated to organizations committed to women's health, family care, and the environment**.

KK lives in New York City and Millbrook, New York with her family. She continues to travel, reporting on lifestyle and fashion on **What2WearWhere.com**.

The Illustrator

Lara Glaister grew up in New York City, where she currently lives. She attended Hobart and William Smith Colleges and after graduation also studied at Parson's School of Design. Always having an urge to channel her creative side, Lara started out in the Contemporary Art world and has since moved on to work in both fashion and media design. Her outlets from city-life include philanthropy and dancing to live music, preferable wearing a feathered-headress in a sari surrounded by palm trees.

EVENT

DESTINATION: _____

LENGTH OF STAY: _____

WEATHER: _____

TIME ZONE: _____

CURRENCY: _____

LIST OF EVENTS/ACTIVITIES:

_____

_____

_____

_____

_____

_____

_____

_____

_____

_____

_____

_____

_____

_____

_____

_____

_____

_____

_____

NOTES FOLLOWING TRIP:

_____

_____

_____

_____

_____

_____

_____

YOUR PACKING LIST

This is your packing list worksheet. Please refer to our various packing lists for guidance.

DAY:

_____

_____

_____

_____

_____

_____

_____

EVENING:

_____

_____

_____

_____

_____

_____

SHOES:

_____

_____

_____

ACCESSORIES:

_____

_____

_____

_____

EVENT

DESTINATION: _____

LENGTH OF STAY: _____

WEATHER: _____

TIME ZONE: _____

CURRENCY: _____

LIST OF EVENTS/ACTIVITIES:

_____

_____

_____

_____

_____

_____

_____

_____

_____

_____

_____

_____

_____

_____

_____

_____

_____

NOTES FOLLOWING TRIP:

_____

_____

_____

_____

_____

_____

_____

YOUR PACKING LIST

This is your packing list worksheet. Please refer to our various packing lists for guidance.

DAY:

_____

_____

_____

_____

_____

_____

_____

EVENING:

_____

_____

_____

_____

_____

_____

_____

SHOES:

_____

_____

_____

_____

ACCESSORIES:

_____

_____

_____

_____

EVENT

DESTINATION: _____

LENGTH OF STAY: _____

WEATHER: _____

TIME ZONE: _____

CURRENCY: _____

LIST OF EVENTS/ACTIVITIES:

_____

_____

_____

_____

_____

_____

_____

_____

_____

_____

_____

_____

_____

_____

_____

_____

_____

NOTES FOLLOWING TRIP:

_____

_____

_____

_____

_____

_____

YOUR PACKING LIST

This is your packing list worksheet. Please refer to our various packing lists for guidance.

DAY:

_____

_____

_____

_____

_____

_____

_____

EVENING:

_____

_____

_____

_____

_____

_____

SHOES:

_____

_____

_____

_____

ACCESSORIES:

_____

_____

_____

_____

Event

DESTINATION: _____

LENGTH OF STAY: _____

WEATHER: _____

TIME ZONE: _____

CURRENCY: _____

LIST OF EVENTS/ACTIVITIES:

_____

_____

_____

_____

_____

_____

_____

_____

_____

_____

_____

_____

_____

_____

_____

_____

_____

NOTES FOLLOWING TRIP:

_____

_____

_____

_____

_____

_____

YOUR PACKING LIST

This is your packing list worksheet. Please refer to our various packing lists for guidance.

DAY:

_____

_____

_____

_____

_____

_____

_____

EVENING:

_____

_____

_____

_____

_____

_____

SHOES:

_____

_____

_____

ACCESSORIES:

_____

_____

_____

_____

EVENT

DESTINATION: _____

LENGTH OF STAY: _____

WEATHER: _____

TIME ZONE: _____

CURRENCY: _____

LIST OF EVENTS/ACTIVITIES:

_____

_____

_____

_____

_____

_____

_____

_____

_____

_____

_____

_____

_____

_____

_____

_____

_____

_____

NOTES FOLLOWING TRIP:

_____

_____

_____

_____

_____

_____

_____

YOUR PACKING LIST

This is your packing list worksheet. Please refer to our various packing lists for guidance.

DAY:

_____

_____

_____

_____

_____

_____

_____

EVENING:

_____

_____

_____

_____

_____

_____

SHOES:

_____

_____

_____

ACCESSORIES:

_____

_____

_____

_____